Archaeology and Ancient Cultures

UNCOVERING THE CULTURE OF
ANCIENT PERU

By Alix Wood

PowerKiDS
press

NEW YORK

Published in 2016 by
The Rosen Publishing Group, Inc.
29 East 21ˢᵗ Street, New York, NY 10010

Cataloging-in-Publication Data

Wood, Alix.
Uncovering the culture of ancient Peru / by Alix Wood.
p. cm. — (Archaeology and ancient cultures)
Includes index.
ISBN 978-1-5081-4667-4 (pbk.)
ISBN 978-1-5081-4668-1 (6-pack)
ISBN 978-1-5081-4669-8 (library binding)
1. Indians of South America — Peru — Juvenile literature. 2. Peru — Antiquities — Juvenile literature.
3. Peru — Juvenile literature. I. Wood, Alix. II. Title.
F3429.W66 2016
980.4—d23

Editor: Eloise Macgregor
Designer: Alix Wood
Consultant: Rupert Matthews

Photo Credits: Cover, 1 © Shutterstock; 2, 10 right, 11 top © Andrew Kunkle; 5 top, 6, 7 bottom, 12 main image, 13 top, 20, 22, 23, 27 © DollarPhotoClub; 5 bottom, 13 bottom, 15 bottom, 19 © Trustees of the British Museum; 7 top © Corbis Images; 8, 9, 24, 28 bottom © AgainErick;12 inset © NASA; 14 © Martin St-Amant; 15 middle © David Almeida; 16 top © M. Moss; 16 bottom © A. Augustus Healy Fund/Brooklyn Museum; 17 top © Templar 1307; 17 bottom, 18 © Howard Smith; 21 top © Tyler Bell; 21 bottom left © Sally Taylor; 21 bottom right © Kevin Stan; 25 © Brien Foerster; 26 bottom © Dyane Plumly; 29 top and bottom © cammaert; 29 © Ministry of Culture; all other images are in the public domain

Manufactured in the United States of America

CPSIA Compliance Information: Batch #: BW16PK For Further Information contact Rosen Publishing, New York, New York at 1-800-237-9932

CONTENTS

ANCIENT PERU

Ancient Peru is probably best known for its Inca Empire. There were other **civilizations** before the Inca, though. The Norte Chico of Peru were the first civilization to form in the Americas. The Chavin civilization followed, in west central Peru. The Nazca civilization developed along the southern coast of Peru, at the same time as the Moche civilization developed along the northern coast of Peru. Both were famous for their pottery. Later, the Wari civilization developed **terraced** farming and a road system.

In the 1100s, the Inca tribe under their leader, Manco Capac began to gain power. The Chimu Empire was conquered by the Inca in 1476 CE. The Spanish arrived in 1531, conquering the Inca and ruling Peru until 1821.

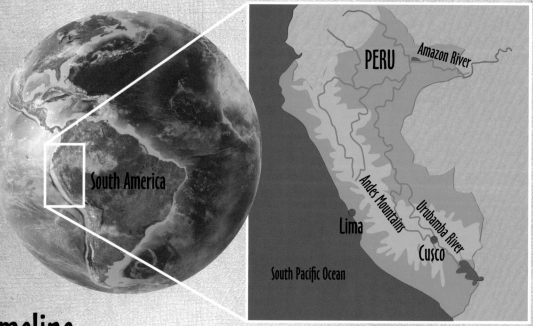

South America

PERU
Amazon River
Andes Mountains
Urubamba River
Lima
Cusco
South Pacific Ocean

Timeline

A colored band by the page number shows each site's time period

c 3000-c 2,500 BCE	c 900 - 200 BCE	100 BCE - 800 CE	100 - 700 CE
Norte Chico	Chavin	Nazca	Moche

The Inca ruins of Machu Picchu
high in the Andes Mountains

One of the strange things about the early civilizations in Peru is that they never used wheels to help transport things. Almost all other early civilizations used wheels. When you look at the steep mountains of the Andes, it may explain why. The people of ancient Peru also never developed a written language. This is also very unusual. Instead they relied on spoken language and drawn images on objects such as pottery to communicate.

Artifact Facts

With no written language, the ancient Peruvians invented this tool to record things on. The quipu is a series of colored, knotted strings. The type of knot and its position signified a number. All the cords hung from a main string, and each cord's position and color probably indicated what was being counted, such as gold, corn, or people.

500 - 1000 CE	1100 - 1470 CE	1200 - 1533 CE
Wari	Chimu	Inca

5

THE FIRST CIVILIZATION

Caral-Supe

The **sacred** city of Caral-Supe was built on a flat area of desert overlooking the Supe river valley in the Norte Chico region of Peru. Caral-Supe is the oldest center of civilization in the Americas. The Norte Chico civilization is sometimes also called the Caral-Supe civilization after its capital. The civilization flourished between around 3000 to 1800 BCE.

When Peruvian **archaeologists** began to **excavate** the city, unusually, they found no pottery and not much art. They didn't find any evidence of warfare either – no defensive walls, weapons, or skeletons with violent injuries. However archaeologists did find the remains of incredible architecture. The Norte Chico built large earthwork mounds and unusual sunken circular public areas. The people must have had an organized society to be able to build projects such as these.

A large sunken plaza found at Caral-Supe

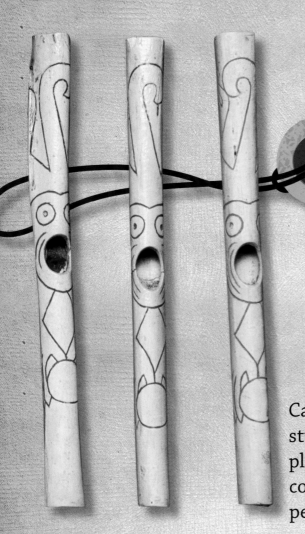

Artifact Facts

The most surprising finds at Caral-Supe were 32 flutes made of condor and pelican bones, and 37 cornets made of deer and llama bones! The musical instruments are around 4,200 years old. These flutes were played by blowing into the central hole and covering either the left or right hand holes.

Archaeologists believe that the people of Caral-Supe were peaceful, and spent their time studying the stars, praying to their gods, and playing on musical instruments. The flutes and cornets were found in a circular plaza. Perhaps people gathered there to listen to music?

This standing stone below is believed to have been used a little like a **sundial**, to work out the time of day. It may also have been used in ceremonies, and to help study the stars. It sits exactly north of one of the pyramids, and the top of the stone and the top of the pyramid line up with the sun at the summer and winter **solstices**.

CUMBE MAYO

Cumbe Mayo

Cumbe Mayo was built by the Norte Chico civilization around 1,500 BCE. "Cumbe Mayo" means "thin river" in the local language, Quechua. It is called this because Cumbe Mayo is best known for the ruins of an ancient **aqueduct**, approximately five miles (8 km) in length. It is thought to be one of the oldest man-made structures in South America.

The aqueduct at Cumbe Mayo

Archaeologists aren't sure why the aqueducts were built, but it was probably to control the flow of water from the melting snow in the hills down to the fields below. The skills needed to build the canals were very advanced. The volcanic rock was probably cut using hammers made from a hard stone called **obsidian**.

Towering above the Cumbe Mayo is a rock formation known as the Friars. It is called this because the rocks look like a group of monks in a procession! The **volcanic** pillars are not man-made, but created by wind and rain wearing away the rock. Man has left his mark there though. One cliff, known as the Sanctuary, looks a little like a man's head. The "mouth" is a small cave, where interesting pictures have been carved into the stone.

The Friars at Cumbe Mayo

The "mouth" of the Sanctuary

Artifact Facts

Pictures carved in stone are called **petroglyphs**. This carved stone is believed to have been used as a ceremonial altar. Some experts think the petroglyphs could tell a story, or they could even be maps around the maze of the forest of rocks.

CHAVÍN DE HUÁNTAR

The settlement at Chavín de Huántar was built where the Mosna and the Huanchecsa rivers join. The area where two rivers meet may have had some religious meaning to the Chavin peoples. A meeting of rivers is known as a "tinkuy," which means a happy meeting of opposite forces. The archaeological site of Chavín gave its name to the culture that developed between 1500 and 300 BCE.

Chavín de Huántar

The Raimondi Stela (right) found at Chavín de Huántar is a carved stone which stands taller than a man. It is believed to be a sacred object to the Chavin civilization. The carving can be viewed either way up! Right-side-up it shows a god in a headdress, holding two tall cacti. Upside-down, the god looks like a smiling jaguar and the headdress turns into a column of smiling faces! Turn the book upside down and see.

This drawing of the stela makes the design clearer.

Tunnels beneath the temple

A temple at the site is built on top of a maze of tunnels. With no windows, the underground passageways are in darkness. Smaller tunnels let air pass through. Archaeologists studying the tunnels believe they might have been used to project sounds! It is possible the whole building could "speak" to any people gathered outside, as if their god was talking to them from under the temple!

Artifact Facts

At the center of the maze of tunnels archaeologists found this tall, carved stone. It is hard to see what the carving is, until you trace both sides of the stone and open out the drawing (right) and a Chavin god appears!

MYSTERIOUS NAZCA

Nazca

In 1940, American historian Paul Kosok was flying over the Nazca Desert studying ancient water systems. He looked down and spotted the shape of an enormous bird drawn in the sand. The ancient, mysterious lines were created between 500 BCE and 500 CE. The figures range from very simple lines to pictures of hummingbirds, spiders, monkeys, and lizards!

The lines were made by removing the desert's red pebbles to reveal the paler ground beneath. Archaeologists are not sure why the Nazca people made the lines, but most believe it was for religious reasons. Recently, sandstorms have uncovered new designs of a snake, a bird, and a llama!

The Nazca Lines seen from a satellite in space.

lines

A photograph of a hummingbird design in the Nazca Desert, taken from an aircraft

The Chauchilla cemetery near Nazca is the only archaeological site in Peru where ancient **mummies** can be seen in their original graves, along with ancient artifacts. The bodies are preserved by the dry, desert weather. The mummies were clothed in embroidered cotton, painted with a **resin**, and kept in tombs made from mud bricks. The resin is thought to have kept out insects and slowed **bacteria** trying to feed on the bodies. Nearby at Estaquería, archaeologists found wooden pillars which they believe were used to dry bodies on, as part of the mummification process.

This thousand-year-old Chauchilla mummy still has hair and the remains of skin!

Artifact Facts

The Nazca produced beautiful ceramics and textiles. Major pottery shapes include double-spout bottles like this one. This hummingbird design is very similar to the design on the Nazca Line opposite.

The Nazca also built underground aqueducts that still function today. When Kosok discovered the Nazca Lines, he was actually investigating the amazing aqueducts! The underground channels bring water from the Andes to the desert.

TEMPLES TO THE MOON AND SUN

Cerro Blanco

The Moche civilization lived in northern Peru from around 100 to 800 CE. They grew crops and built irrigation canals to supply water. They created beautiful painted pottery, gold work, and built monumental temples known as "huaca." At their capital, Cerro Blanco, the Moche built several large mud-brick temples including the Huaca de la Luna (the temple of the Moon) and Huaca del Sol (the temple of the Sun).

The Huaca del Sol was damaged and looted by Spanish conquistadors in the 17th century. The Huaca de la Luna was left mostly untouched. It was decorated in murals painted in black, bright red, sky blue, white, and yellow. Under its central platform archaeologists have found several important burials of what they believe were priests. The grave goods found at the Huaca del Sol suggest the burials there may have been of political rulers.

A wall at the Huaca de la Luna. Known as "the Decapitator," this spider god is often pictured with a knife in one hand, and a human head in the other!

Many of the walls at Cerro Blanco show the Moche god, Ayapec. Ayapec means "all-knowing."

Huaca de la Luna, in front of the volcanic mountain, Cerro Blanco, after which the town was named.

The Moche sacrificed people during rituals. Many of their ceramics have images of **sacrifices**. The bodies of victims would be thrown over the side of the temple and left on the ground below. Archaeologists have found many skeletons of adult males at the foot of one rock, most of whom show signs of a severe blow to the head as their cause of death!

Artifact Facts

This pottery vase is typical of some of the beautiful Moche ceramics. They painted their pottery with colored "slip," a watered-down clay, and then fired the pot. They needed to be very skilled to work out what color the slip would turn once it was fired. This flute player was found at nearby Trujillo.

PIKILLAQTA

Pikillaqta

The Wari lived in the south-central Andes and coastal area of Peru, from about 500 to 1000 CE. They invaded some areas of the earlier Moche culture, also. The Wari culture began to disappear around 800 CE, probably because of a **drought**. Archaeologists have found buildings in the Wari cities had their doorways deliberately blocked up, as if the Wari intended to come back when the rains returned.

Pikillaqta was a large Wari settlement with a fresh water supply, and an underground sewage system. The Wari were the first to develop a way of growing crops on the hillsides by creating areas of flat terrace. To water the terraces, they built over 30 miles (48 km) of canals!

Llamas graze on terraces where the Wari would have grown their crops.

Artifact Facts

The Wari grew corn and potatoes, and raised llama and alpaca. They used the wool from the llama and alpaca to make hats such as this one. They traded their textiles and ceramics across the Andes. The Wari created a network of roads to link their cities and trade routes.

All Wari cities are alike, designed with narrow streets laid out in a grid pattern. Oddly, the streets at Pikillaqta had few windows, and hardly any doorways! There was no obvious way in or out of the city, either. Archaeologists have only found one narrow passage that ran along an outside wall leading to a small entrance. This would have helped keep out any unwanted visitors!

With tall walls and no windows, it would have been very difficult to find a way out of Pikillaqta.

Experts think the buildings may have been storerooms rather than houses. **Ancestor** worship was a tradition, and people kept the bones of their dead relatives so they could ask them for blessings and advice. The Wari may have captured other peoples' mummies and stored them at Pikillaqta! Archaeologists found bone fragments with copper stains but no copper was found nearby. They believe this means the bones had been moved to Pikillaqta.

One of the long streets at Pikillaqta

PACHACAMAC

Pachacamac

Pachacamac was an important city in the Lurín River valley. It was built by the Wari culture around 800-1450 CE. The city was then taken by the Inca Empire, who added buildings of their own. Archaeologists have discovered remains of 17 pyramids! There is also a cemetery and a much earlier multicolored **fresco** of fish from around 200-600 CE.

Pachacamac was a religious site, with a temple built to the Wari creator god, Pacha Kamaq. Pacha Kamaq was feared as a bringer of earthquakes. Priests would ask the god questions and give the answers to the crowds waiting outside. The invading Inca let the priests continue doing this, but added their own temple to the Sun on the main square.

A carving of the god Pacha Kamaq. Priests were said to enter the temple backward, so they did not have to look at the terrifying statue!

The ruins of Pachacamac

The carved Pacha Kamaq idol was discovered by Dr. Alberto Giesecke in 1938. The statue has two faces looking in opposite directions. On one side his clothing is decorated with corn, and on the other side, with animal figures.

Workers unearthing the early fish fresco in 1938.

During Giesecke's 1938 excavation of the Old Temple, an unusual gate was found. Back in 1533, Spanish writer Miguel de Estete described a temple entrance that the Spanish found as being woven with different objects such as coral, turquoise, valuable shells, and crystals. The door Giesecke found was made out of a base of wooden sticks bound together by white rope. The door was then covered by a plain fabric onto which objects such as shells were sewn!

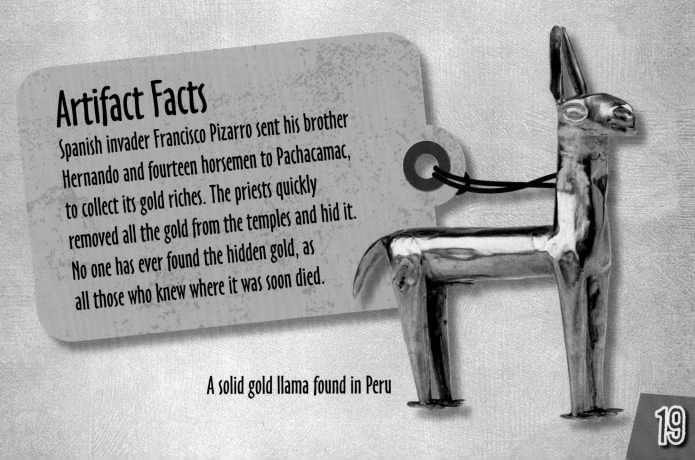

Artifact Facts

Spanish invader Francisco Pizarro sent his brother Hernando and fourteen horsemen to Pachacamac, to collect its gold riches. The priests quickly removed all the gold from the temples and hid it. No one has ever found the hidden gold, as all those who knew where it was soon died.

A solid gold llama found in Peru

SACSAYHUAMAN

Sacsayhuaman

Sacsayhuaman is a citadel on the outskirts of the city of Cusco, capital of the Inca Empire. The settlement was first built in 1100, and was expanded by the Inca from the 1200s. The Inca builders were incredibly skillful. The walls were built using huge stones which the workers carefully cut. The boulders fit together exactly without any need for **mortar**.

The plaza at Sacsayhuaman has three massive terrace walls (below). The stones used to build these terraces are enormous and so closely spaced that even a sheet of paper will not fit between them!

The stones' interlocking shapes, and the fact that the walls and doorways are built leaning inward have helped the ruins survive many earthquakes.

The Inca first cut the stones to a rough shape at the quarry. Then the stones were dragged by rope to the building site, often needing many men to haul each one. The stones were then cut into their final shape and laid in place. Archaeologists aren't sure how they cut the stones, as no metal hard enough is thought to have been invented at the time. The cut stone was hauled up a ramp above where it was to fit, and put on top of a stack of logs. The logs would then be removed one by one to lower the stone into place.

Inca buildings often had **niches** in walls, like this one at Sacsayhuaman. Large niches may have been used for attendants to stand in, but most were probably used to display important items.

Artifact Facts

There are images of a llama, a puma's paw (below), and a snake (right) in the rocks at Sacsayhuaman. This snake is believed to have been filled with gold.

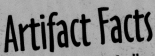

OLLANTAYTAMBO

Ollantaytambo was the royal estate of Inca emperor Pachacuti. During the Spanish conquest of Peru, the settlement housed the leader of the Inca resistance, Manco Inca. He fortified the town and defeated a Spanish army there. Then Manco Inca fled, and Ollantaytambo was taken by the Spanish.

In peaceful times, Ollantaytambo was a farming center. Stone terracing made the steep hillside into usable crop land. The terraces gave level ground for farming, and helped prevent landslides after heavy rains. Above the growing areas, the Inca built grain stores which could store up to a five-year supply of emergency food. Crops were planted at different altitudes to get the best growing conditions. For example, hundreds of different types of potatoes were grown, and each variety needed different conditions.

Ollantaytambo

The growing terraces at Ollantaytambo

The skilled Inca craftsmen who created this incredible jigsaw of rock never used wheels to help transport their heavy stone. Why not?

The Inca cities were built on steep slopes. Carrying goods on pack animals, such as llamas, was much easier than dragging a wagon up a mountain. Some experts believe the Inca never used wheels because the shape represented the sacred Sun and Moon, and shouldn't be used for everyday tasks. At Ollantaytambo, archaeologists have found evidence that the Inca built long, complex ramps to help drag the stone from the quarries to the site.

Artifact Facts

The Princess Bath at Ollantaytambo was for **ceremonial** bathing. The princess knelt under the flow of water. If she ran her fingers across the spout, the flow of water would stop! By flicking water back at the spout, the water would start flowing again.

The Princess Bath has a basin at the top, shaped so the water spun around inside. They put sand in the **whirlpool** to filter the water!

STRANGE ROCKS

Saywite was a center of worship for the Inca people, focusing on water. The temple priestess, Asarpay, is said to have jumped into a nearby gorge to her death to avoid being captured by the Spanish.

Saywite has a most incredible secret that no archaeologist has yet understood. A mysterious carved rock lies on top of a hillside there. It has over 200 geometric shapes and animal figures carved into it. The stone looks like an Inca city, complete with stairs, and water channels. Archaeologists are not sure what the rock was for. Some experts believe the rock was used as a **scale model** to test water irrigation. Others think it may have been used in ceremonies that worshiped water.

The Saywite monolith is 7.5 feet (2.3 m) tall.

Another large stone at Saywite (below) has beautifully carved stairs. It has cracked in half, probably from being struck by lightning or from earthquake damage. No one is sure what this stone was for, either. It is possible the three large steps symbolize the three levels of the Inca universe; the upper world of the gods, the world of everyday existence, and the underworld inhabited by spirits of the dead. One theory is that the stone was used at wedding ceremonies. The couple would kneel on the steps and be blessed by sacred water from bowl-shaped holes found carved into the top platform.

MACHU PICCHU

Machu Picchu

Machu Picchu is an abandoned Inca city, high up in the Andes mountains above the Urubamba River. It was abandoned during the Spanish Conquest. Over the centuries, routes to the city became overgrown by jungle, and only a few local people knew it existed.

Hiram Bingham was an American historian interested in Inca ruins. In 1911, he organized an expedition down the Urubamba River to search for the last capital of the Incas. A local farmer, Melchor Arteaga, said he knew of some excellent ruins. He led Bingham across the river and up a mountain. They met some farmers using the ancient terraces to grow crops. Pablito, an 11-year-old farmer's son, led Bingham along the ridge to find an amazing sight – Machu Picchu!

Hiram Bingham outside his tent, Machu Picchu, 1912.

Artifact Facts

Carved into the floor of the Temple of the Sun are two of these stone bowls. When filled with water, they act like mirrors. Archaeologists believe the Inca used them to observe the sky. Also, in the temple on the winter solstice, the Sun shines through a specially angled window and lights up a sacred rock inside.

Artifact Facts

This stone is called Intihuatana, which means "the place where the Sun gets tied." During the winter solstice, the Sun is directly overhead and the stone casts no shadow. The solstice, called the Inti Raymi, was one of the Inca's most important celebrations.

Machu Picchu was an excellent place to build Inca emperor Pachacuti's estate. A rope bridge across the Urubamba River provided a secret entrance. Another tree-trunk bridge crossed a dangerous long drop between two cliffs. These two routes could be easily blocked if invaders approached. Machu Picchu had a clear view down two valleys, and a steep mountain behind it. It had spring water and enough land to grow food.

Can you see a man's face in the mountain? The completely natural formation seems to show a face looking up at the sky!

THE RED PLACE

Tambo Colorado

Tambo Colorado is an old Inca city and burial site. Its name means "colorful place." The site was most likely built during the reign of the Inca king Pachacutec. Many of the walls are painted with horizontal strips of red, black, white, and yellow. The very dry conditions at Tambo meant that when Peruvian archaeologist Julio Tello discovered the site, much of the colorful paint on the walls had been preserved.

Tambo Colorado is thought to have been an important center for passing traffic on the road to Cusco. It was also where Inca runners waited to relay messages. Fast runners waited at stations every 4.2 miles (7 km) across Peru, so that messages could be passed from one end of the country to the other in just 24 hours!

Peruvian archaeologist Julio Tello discovered Tambo Colorado beneath sand dunes in 1925.

Tambo Colorado is built using local mud brick. Some Inca building styles, along with the local methods were used. Niches in the walls at Tambo Colorado (left) were narrower at the top as is typical in Inca buildings. The niches were probably used to house important objects.

As with all Inca buildings, these niches are exactly the same size and shape across the site.

In May 2014, archaeologists working at Tambo Colorado discovered a secret **mural** created before the arrival of the Spanish in Peru. It is typical of the local Chincha-Inca style and was discovered hidden under a layer of white plaster. It's possible the mural's creators covered it to protect their work from being destroyed by the invading Spanish!

The hidden mural

Artifact Facts

A museum at the site houses many of Tello's cemetery finds. Several skulls show signs of a medical procedure where a metal plate was used to replace broken areas of skull!

GLOSSARY

ancestor A relative who lived long ago.

aqueduct A channel or pipe used to carry water for long distances.

archaeologists Scientists that study past human life, fossils, monuments and tools left by ancient peoples.

bacteria Tiny living things that cannot be seen with the eye alone. Some bacteria cause illness or rotting, but others are helpful.

ceremonial Having to do with a ceremony, or series of actions done for special occasions.

civilizations People living in an organized way.

drought A period of dryness that causes harm to crops.

excavate To dig up something that was buried.

fresco A painting done on wet plaster.

mortar A mixture of lime, cement, sand and water for holding bricks or stones together.

mummies Bodies prepared for burial in a way that makes them last a long time.

mural Pictures painted on a wall.

niches A hollowed-out place in a wall especially for a statue.

obsidian A hard dark, glassy rock formed by the cooling of molten lava.

petroglyphs Writings or figures cut into rock.

resin A sticky liquid obtained from the gum or sap of some trees.

sacred Set apart in honor of someone.

sacrifices An act of offering something precious to a god, such as the killing of a victim.

scale model An exact, though smaller, model of something.

solstices The days when the Sun is either farthest north or south of the equator.

sundial A device to show the time of day by the position of the shadow cast.

terraced Made of raised, steplike banks of earth.

volcanic From a volcano.

whirlpool Water that moves quickly in a circle.

FURTHER INFORMATION

Books

Aveni, Anthony. *Buried Beneath Us: Discovering the Ancient Cities of the Americas*. New York, NY: Roaring Book Press, 2013.

Lewin, Ted. *Lost City: The Discovery of Machu Picchu*. London, UK: Puffin Books, 2012.

Steele, Philip. *Hands-On History! Incas*. London, UK: Armadillo, 2014.

Waldron, Melanie. *Geography Matters in the Inca Empire*. Basingstoke, UK: Raintree, 2015.

Due to the changing nature of Internet links, PowerKids Press has developed an online list of websites related to the subject of this book. This site is updated regularly. Please use this link to access the list:

www.powerkidslinks.com/AAC/Peru

INDEX